The Sweetest Little Blueberry

Cheyenne Bluett

BOOKS BY THIS AUTHOR

Poetry
His Green Eyes
Bright Yellow Sunshine
Dark Blue Waves
The Moon Sends Her Love
Magic All Along

Paranormal Romance
(Pandora Bluett)
Wicked Transcendence

CHEYENNE BLUETT

For Lylah.

I love you.

I stare at the test,
my future blossoming
before my eyes
all because of
two pink lines.

Fear and joy
and disbelief and excitement
simultaneously
zap through my veins
as I realize what this means.

I'm pregnant.

I am somehow able
to keep this secret
from your daddy
all day.

I want to make sure
I *really am* pregnant,
so I stop by the store
after work
and I take three more tests
(to triple check)
and they all reveal
their own sets
of two pink lines
(three times).

Confirming
yes, I'm pregnant.

I wait
all bubbly inside
for him to get home.
Of course he's home late today!
When the time is right,
I finally show him
those two pink lines
(four times).

Oh my gosh.
        He said.
Yeah.
        I said.

We smile at each other
as our future becomes clear.
We are parents now
a baby on the way
a new life joining ours.

As we embrace with tears in our eyes,
we vow to always remember this moment
and how our life changed
all because of
two pink lines.

Hi, baby.
I know we are technically strangers,
but I want to tell you something.

This world will be so much better with you in it.

How do I explain the feeling
of pure love,
pure joy,
pure pride I feel
when I think about you
and the moment
we will finally meet?

You hear my innermost thoughts.
You eat all the snacks I do.
I feel you move inside me,
and I know you hear my voice.

I know you inside and out
and you know me the same
but someday I'll know you
even *more*.

I can't wait until
the day I hold you in my arms
and meet you
officially.

LOVE AT FIRST SIGHT

I nervously pick at my fingernails,
sitting in the doctor's waiting room.

Today is the day
I see you
for the first time.

I am excited and nervous
and ready but not.
I have thought of this moment
since I scheduled this appointment
weeks ago
and now here I am
hopeful to know
everything is alright
but terrified to know
that it's not.

Finally, they call my name.

My heart pounds in my ears
as I follow the nurse.
She takes my blood pressure
and bombards me with questions,
and I try to focus
but I'm trembling with anticipation.
I'm shaking so bad
I almost pee on my hand
instead of in the tiny cup.

The nurse ushers me
into the dark room
with the sonogram machine,
and I sit in the chair,
watching the tech
with wide eyes
as she types on her computer,

oblivious to my anxiety.

"Breathe, sweetie."
my love says to me,
holding my hand.
He can feel how shaky I am,
so he gives me reassuring squeezes
and rubs his thumb across mine.

But how does he know?
What if there's no heartbeat?

I lift my shirt
per the tech's instructions,
exposing my stomach
and giggling nervously
when the cold gel is slathered on.

Without a warning,
the wand is now gliding
across my flat abdomen,
where there might someday be
a big baby bump.

I stare at the screen in front of me,
not daring to breathe,
as she tries to find my baby.

With each passing second
my anxiety threatens
to cut off my lungs entirely,
but then

but then

there
you
are.

"There's your baby."

My hand flies to my mouth
as a sob escapes my lips.

"And here's their heartbeat."

I close my eyes
as the sound echoes around the room,
like a horse galloping

thumpthumpthumpthumpthump

and when I look to my love
your dad
he is smiling so big.

We leave with pictures
of our tiny little baby,
about the size of a blueberry.

We tack the picture onto the fridge
the second we get home
and lean into each other
as we stare at the little blob.

There's a heartbeat.
There's our baby.

The sweetest little blueberry.

This is not the first time I've been pregnant.

I was one other time before,
but by the time
I got over the surprise
and started feeling excited,
the shock returned
with devastation
as I miscarried.

Being pregnant again
brings such fear
and worry,
and I try to remind myself
over and over again
that this is a different pregnancy
and I should have hope
that this little blueberry will make it
safely into my arms,
but I can't stop remembering
all the blood from before…

I told myself
I didn't want to
lessen the gift of you
with my fear
of losing you.

I haven't been successful.

How can I fully immerse myself
in love for this baby
when I am still, always going to
grieve the baby
who died in my womb?

Am I a bad mother
because it breaks my heart
to remember
the life I imagined
is still going to happen,
just now with a different baby?

Miscarriage does more
than take away a life,
it ruins the naiveness of a perfect pregnancy.

Now, I will always have the fear
of loss
buzzing in the back of my mind.
Even when this new baby
is perfectly healthy
and the doctor says everything is fine...
is it?

Things could go wrong so easily.

How can I just pretend
that everything is okay
when a part of me
will always remember
the feeling of being fine
and then *not*
just a moment later?

I love you,
little one,
but if you could stop
making me feel
so yucky all the time
that would be great.

It's hard for me to fully love you
because I am so afraid to lose you.

I know it's unfair
and I'm sorry.

Each day we get through
I open my heart
a tiny bit more,
allowing myself
to fall for you slowly.

I promise I will love you entirely someday…

I keep
drop
drop
dropping weight
because you hate
every single thing I eat.

Morning sickness
has become
all-day sickness,
and I never thought
I could throw up this much.

Running to the bathroom at work,
pulling over to the side of the road
and hurrying to find an old plastic grocery bag,
waking at 2am
and trying to be quiet
so I don't wake your daddy.

I've tried everything I could
soup and preggy pops
pressure bands
and snacking on crackers
and ginger
and every single thing
recommended to me
by other mothers

and yet
nothing's working.

You sure are stubborn,
aren't you,
little one?

Your little fingers and toes
and arms and nose
I cannot wait
to bathe in kisses.

Becoming a mother is not only good feelings.
There is fear and anxiety as well.

Did I make the right choice in getting pregnant?
Have you seen the world right now?
Was I selfish to bring a child into this mess?

Was I selfish enough before getting pregnant?
Will I regret not traveling more?
Will I wish I had more time?

What if I don't like being a mom?
What if my baby doesn't like me?

There are so many things that can go wrong.
What if having a baby is just one big mistake?

Then I take a deep breathe
and think of the positives.

What if I find a kind of happiness I've never known?
What if I am filled with joy, even on the hardest nights?
What will it be like to rock you to sleep?
What will it be like to hear you laugh for the first time?
Will you like to dance?
Will you dance with me?
What if I love being a mother?

Being pregnant is hard.

You must sacrifice your body
and your mental health
and your life
and not complain
because it's what we were *made* to do.

Who came up with the rule
that you aren't allowed
to vocalize
how painful and traumatic
pregnancy can be?

Shots and blood draws
and depression
high blood pressure
and painful cramps
IV treatments
and shaken leg syndrome
and *even more.*

Sometimes pregnancy sucks.

Planning your arrival
takes up a lot of my time,
the anticipation making me
anxious in all the good ways

but I know nothing can compare
to what life will be like
when you are actually here.

I worry about you often.
I just want you to be okay.
I finally understand
The Mother's Love,
how I'd sacrifice everything
even my own life
if it would mean
you will be alright.

I'm finally allowing myself to feel love for you
little stranger in my belly,
and words cannot accurately describe
how much I do love you.

The most giggle-inducing experience
is when you have the hiccups.
I feel them in my belly,
you jumping consistently
for a few minutes at a time.

Keep practicing your breathing,
little one.
You got this.

"I think the baby just kicked me!"
She giggled,
her hand flying to her belly.

"Really?!" he asked.

"Come here, give me your hand."

He walked over and stuck his hand under hers
and they waited.

Right as they were about to give up,
it happened again.

The faintest kick of an itty-bitty foot.

They smiled at each other.
"She's getting strong."

How can I love
and cherish
and appreciate
and support
my own children
when I struggle to do
these things
for myself?

I crave things I've never eaten before
and I hate things I used to love.
Being pregnant is so weird,
but thank you for introducing me
to French fries smothered in honey mustard,
and pickles every second of the day.
I'm sad I don't like pizza anymore,
and wish I could enjoy coffee like I used to,
but I know that someday
my tastebuds will be normal again.

Hopefully.

I knew without a doubt in my mind
what you were.

Even before we found out for sure
I always knew
you were my little girl.

We've both had many titles in our lives.
Some separate and some together.

Man.
Woman.

You.
Me.

Us.

Girlfriend.
Boyfriend.

Fiancé.

Husband.
Wife.

Now...

Mom.
Dad.

Our nursery furniture
was delivered today.
We giggled the entire time
we set it all up.

I made your dad pose for pictures
and pause so I could document the entire thing.
Even though he rolled his eyes a few times,
I caught him smiling when his back was turned to me.

We are so, so excited for the day you sleep in your crib
or use your changing table for the first time.

It seems so far away
until we look at the calendar
and remember
how soon it actually is.

!!!!!

I put my hand on my stomach,
and you always respond with a kick.
I take that as a
"Hello, mommy!"
and it brings a smile to my lips every time.

Hello, baby.

I melt into
one thousand tiny droplets
whenever your daddy
kisses my belly
and whispers sweet secrets to you.

Even as you grow
into the size
of a bigger fruit or veggie,
you'll always be
my little blueberry.

Though my changing body terrifies me,
I know it is all worth it.

Though my once cute
pink perky nipples
are now UFO's sitting
on what feels like cow utters,
I know it is all worth it.

Though stretch marks are appearing
on the ginormous belly
sticking out in front of me,
the same belly that once held abs,
I know it is all worth it.

Though I no longer have ankles
and it hurts to sleep
and I can't tie my shoes
and I cry when I do
Literally anything,
I know it is all worth it.

You are worth it, sweet baby.

I will never get used
to the uncomfortable feeling
of your foot pressed
all the way up in my ribcage.

Sometimes it makes me giggle
watching my belly move
as you wiggle and dance inside me.

Other times it is absolutely terrifying.

They say I will miss these times,
and I know they are right.

I will miss the baby kicks,
and the cute pregnancy outfits,
and the times I rub this big belly
and remember I'm a literal goddess.

But it's okay to also not miss some of it,
like throwing up constantly
and feeling like you got hit by a truck
everything aching,
and bloody noses.

Pregnancy isn't always fun
but can be painful and miserable at times

and it's okay
to only survive the bad days,
remembering they will be over soon.

Baby,
oh, my sweet baby.
I love you.
Do you know that?
I love you, I love you, I love you.

I know you feel it,
since your heart
is beating next to mine.

I love you, I love you, I love you.

I thought I knew every type of love.

I have my loved family my whole life,
this warm feeling in my body
as I hug everyone goodbye.

I have loved my husband since
the moment I said hello,
this feeling in my soul,
happy and crazy and home.

And then I saw your little blob body
on the sonogram
and a love I've never experienced
appeared in my heart.

I cannot explain this new love entirely,
but I assume it's what they say
The Mother's Love is.

Protective and willing
to do whatever in order
to keep my baby safe.
Happy thinking about
who they are, who they will be.
Peace at knowing that
I am the perfect mother for them.

If I love you this much already
without actually meeting you,
I cannot imagine how much my love will grow
even more,
taking up
more room than even possible,
when I finally look into your perfect face.

I have been working on
being able to look in the mirror
without tears flooding to my eyes.

My once taut stomach
smooth and blemish-free
is now round and covered
in dark purple streaks.

Labels of stretch marks
I've heard all my life
ugly
sad
fat
undesirable
crowd my mind.

I can hear women complaining about theirs,
see the ads promoting how to get rid of them
because they are that bad.

I am trying to flip the script
and change my outlook
and admire and cherish
the new "blemishes" I have.

Each stretch mark
is proof
that I created
and carried a life
for nine months.
Proof that my body held
and grew
and nurtured
an actual *human*
with it's own heart and soul
and fingers and toes.

These marks show the months of excitement
anxiety
happiness
memories
and more.

These marks are proof
that I am strong
and I am brave
and I am more beautiful now
than I have ever been.

She had to make room in their bedroom for the bassinet.
She placed it next to her bed,
so night feedings
and early morning diaper changes
would be easier.

She sits on her bed
and stares at the bassinet,
baffled that there will be
a tiny human in it soon.

Her tiny human.

I am to the point of pregnancy where I am
so ready for you to be out.
I can only wear slip-on shoes
because I cannot
bend down
to tie shoelaces
or zip up boots.

I can barely walk four steps
before I get out of breath.

I am so tired
but cannot sleep at night
because my body aches
and you kick me
and wake me
and I literally pee
every hour.

Not to mention the heartburn.
Oh, god, the worst part of it all.

I love you so much,
and I'm so happy you're comfy and happy,
but, please,
come soon?

I am soaking in these last few days
of just you and I,
as close as we will ever be.

Soon you will be out in this world,
not snug in my belly,
and everyone will be able to love you
as much as I do.

Selfishly, I don't want you out
because I don't want anyone else
to love you like I do.

I don't want anyone else to hold you
or kiss you
because I feel like
I am the only one who can keep you safe
and the only one
who can love you this much.

But I know it's okay
that I have to share you sometimes
because at night
we will return to the rocking chair
with the lights off,
just you and I.

I'm sitting in your nursery
surrounded by freshly-washed clothes
and bottles and baby toys,
and tears fill my eyes
as I look around the room.

In such a short time
you will be here.
In this house,
in my arms,
in your daddy's arms,
in our lives.
Wearing the clothes
I'm currently organizing in drawers,
sleeping in the crib
we spent hours picking out and setting up.

I've been praying for this moment
since longer than I could remember,
and it's finally happening
and I cannot believe it.

I almost didn't answer the phone—
I distrust random numbers.

But something inside me
knew it was important,
so I clicked the green button
and brought the phone to my ear.

"Hello?"
"It's induction day!" my nurse squealed.

I called your daddy and told him the news,
and he hurried home,
excited as can be!

I took my time showering,
lathering my belly,
whispering to you
today is the day!

Your daddy and I got donuts
on our way to the hospital,
a celebratory breakfast.

I took pictures all the way there
and then daddy and I kissed each other
in the parking lot
one last time…

"Ready Freddy?"
"Freddy Ready."

CHEYENNE BLUETT

blinding overhead lights
nurses
a blue sheet
a giant needle

n u m b n e s s

the doctor
quiet words
husband holding my hand
a ticking clock

n e r v o u s n e s s

naked on a table
"are you ready?"
a nod
silence…
a newborn cry

j o y

CHEYENNE BLUETT

She's here
and my God,
words cannot describe
her beauty.

I am not even going to try.

Welcome to the world, little one.

I am naked and bleeding
and lying in a hospital bed,
covered in scratchy blankets

guests in the room
cooing over the baby
that has just made her arrival

the love in the room is palpable–
I can see it in our eyes,
feel it in the magic of our bones.

My mother walks to me,
leaning down to kiss my forehead.
"You did it, baby. I am so proud of you."

I close my eyes, fighting tears against her words.

I know the love she is feeling in this moment,
because I am now a mother, too.

How do I put in words
how I understand now,
how much I love her?

When I open my eyes
to find what to say,
you just nod,
knowing what I am feeling
because
of course you do.

I love you, Mom.

Years ago my mother was here,
lying in a similar bed,
staring at people loving her baby.

Here I am doing the same.

Women do this every day
and we pass down the pride
and the adoration and the bliss
of motherhood
as we welcome our new babies into this world.

And I think that someday
I may be in a room like this again,
but the one kissing my daughter's forehead
as she holds her new miracle.

Mothers. Are. Incredible.

The clock on the wall
keeps ticking away
proof that time is moving
and yet I don't even notice.

Your daddy is sleeping
on the couch
and we are illuminated
by the flicker of the tv.

I'm stuck in awe
holding your tiny body
smiling and soaking in
the crazy notion
that you're finally here.

I drink in every cry
and every tiny snore
not even giving my eyes
time to rest
because how could I
at a moment like this?

I can't believe
I am lucky enough
to experience
a moment like this.

I will never forget the night
we created life
and I will never forget
the way you looked
as you held our miracle
in your arms
for the first time.

C-section,
vaginal,
epidural,
spinal tap,
natural,
planned,
scheduled,
emergency,
easy recovery,
tough recovery,
candlelight
traumatic
relaxing...

no matter your birth story,
you did it, Mama.

You gave birth.
You pushed through the pain
you didn't give up,
and you *did it.*
You are so strong
and I am so proud of you.

I remember counting down the days
as every new week passed,
excitedly checking the baby chart
to see how big you were this week.

First a little sprinkle,
and then a blueberry.
a lemon,
and eventually a pumpkin.

And now here you are
no longer a fruit I am imagining
but a little 8 pound human
living and breathing and wrapped in my arms.

I had always imagined what you'd look like
and now my eyes are taking you all in.
A little nose
and two little eyes,
tiny fingers with tiny fingernails
and soft dark hair on smooth new skin.

I am learning who I am in your world.
Mine already existed before you,
but that part of me is now irrelevant.
Now my entire life
revolves around you.
How do I fit my life
into yours?

*I never knew a tiny yawn
could be so adorable.*

I love you more than I ever thought possible;
opening a section of my heart
that I didn't even know existed.

I will do everything in my power
to make sure you never forget how much
I love you.

Times one thousand.
Times one million.
Times infinity.

How could something so small
take up so much room in my heart?
How could something so mini
change my world so monumentally?

This baby is my rainbow baby.
Many women know what that means,
as they too have their own rainbows
and know exactly the pain I feel.

I'm so grateful
for this new love,
but I will never forget
the pain
of losing the baby before her.

The doctor gives us paperwork
and a bag of baby goodies
and lots of mesh underwear
and sends us on our way
with
"Good luck!"

We are home.
Now what?

The first night was the hardest
the waking every few hours
barely able to move
and trying to figure out
how we will survive like this.

Someday I will sleep again... right?

I'm exhausted and I've cried every hour
I'm bleeding down my legs
and leaking out my breasts.
I'm soothing a newborn
on no sleep
and trying not to pass out.
I'm barely able to walk
and I'm sipping water when I can
and I'm crying again because I am so damn exhausted.

And you are begging
to come hold the baby
so I can "get some stuff done."

what if I turn my back for one second and you stop breathing
what if I turn my back for one second and you slip off the bed
what if I turn my back for one second and the dog nips you
what if I turn my back for one second and you choke
what if I turn my back for one second and you cry
what if I turn my back for one second and you suffocate
what if I turn my back for one second and you stop breathing
what if I turn my back for one second and you stop breathing
what if I turn my back for one second and you stop breathing

How do I explain how conflicted I am?

How I want help,
I *need* help
but I cannot imagine anyone else holding my baby.

I want me time
I *need* me time,
but the idea of me being away from her
gives me unbearable anxiety.

I cannot imagine being away from her
what if she needs me?

I am the only one who knows her like I do,
I am the one who feeds her and changes her and loves her
I know how to put her to sleep and what song she likes,
No one else can do it as well as I can
so no one should
so I must stay here with her
forever.

I imagined you
a million different ways,
with blonde hair or red hair
and blue eyes or brown,
dimples and wrinkles and tiny fingernails.

And nothing in my wildest imagination
could have dreamed up
how perfect and beautiful
you actually are.

My phone storage is depleting rapidly
because I cannot stop taking pictures of you.

It's 2:14am.
You are back asleep
after nursing and a diaper change.

I stare at the ceiling,
unable to close my eyes.

A week ago I was lying like this
awake on a table
as they cut you out of me.

I could feel the twinges of hands
and I threw up
and felt nauseous and anxious.
Suddenly there you were,
and I didn't even see you get pulled out.
I didn't even meet you
until minutes later,
you were wrapped up in a blanket
and handed to your dad.
I didn't get the golden hour skin to skin
I couldn't even hold you until a few hours later.

I was shamed by my lactation nurse
for giving you a binky,
and she made me sob because
you were struggling to latch.

The nurses skipped my second medication
and I was in throbbing pain,
crying because of the fresh stitches on my abdomen.

I can't close my eyes
because I can't shake the fear
of being in that room.

Birth Trauma.

Instead of going to a new parents house
to beg to hold the baby,
why not help with the dirty dishes?
Or fold the laundry that's clearly been there for a while?
Or make dinner?

Don't take away the baby
she has spent months growing
and don't get upset
when she says *no, I'm holding **my** baby.*

You didn't check on me once during my pregnancy,
but now you are one of the first ones
to brag about the new baby on social media?

What's wrong with this picture?

I have never felt so unimportant
or that my needs no longer matter
than when I was a new mother
and everyone only wanted to see the baby.

My job is done;
I brought her safely into this world,
and that's all that matters.

Now everyone can love her
like they used to love me,
and I am slowly fading away,
and no one is even noticing.

"Do you have to go?" she whines to her husband,
unwashed hair and sleepless eyes,
cradling the baby that just woke up.

"I have to go to work, dear." he says,
kissing her goodbye
and leaving out the door.

She hears his truck leave
and resentment builds
as she thinks of his day–
with other adults
maybe they'll get lunch together
and then alone time
and brain stimulation
and *everything she desperately needs.*

And then he comes home
and says "I'm so tired from work."

And it takes all her willpower not to snap at him.

At least you get to leave this house
and don't have sore stiches
and eat warm food
and have alone time
and don't listen to a baby's cry
and...

But she only smiles
and says
"Welcome home."

Nothing prepares you
for the aching of your heart
when you hear your baby cry.

Even if it's just for a few minutes,
while you change their diaper
or heat their bottle,
it still brings tears to your eyes.

I rock you to sleep
              and I nurse you
                           and I change you
and I rock you to sleep
              and I nurse you
                           and I change you

and the days blur together
and it seems that all I do lately

is rock you to sleep
              and nurse you
                           and change you
and rock you to sleep
              and nurse you
                           and change you

Every two hours
you latch onto me
and it hurts
and it's exhausting
and it's so much work
and even though I won't stop
I wish I would've known
how much work
and how difficult
breastfeeding is.

Nipple creams
and ice packs
and pump parts
and latching
and relatching
and
ouch
ouch
ouch.

I am not a good mother.

I cannot do this.

Why did I ever think I could?

How can I love and take care of a baby?

She will be better off without me.

How can I love and take care of a baby and myself?

I am so tired.

Why did I ever think I could do this?

I cannot.

I am not a good mother.

Change her.
Feed her.
Play with her.
Rock her until she sleeps.

By the time that's over,
you have an hour
until you do it all again.
An hour for you to do
those things you've been wanting...
like brush your hair.
Eat something.
Take a nap.
But you are so exhausted
that all you can do
is sit on the couch
and mindlessly scroll your phone
or so anxious
that you check the monitor
every five minutes
to make sure she's breathing
and get so enamored
that you watch her until
she starts stirring awake.

Then the cycle repeats:
change, feed, play, sleep.

Not including extra pumping sessions,
or outfit changes,
or baths,
or those times all the baby wants to do is cry.

Change, feed, play, sleep.

Until you realize it's now 10pm
and you haven't eaten all day,
and people think they are being nice
when they say

"you don't even look like you've had a baby!"
when you drop thirty pounds in a month.
When it reality,
you are too busy taking care of the baby
to take care of yourself.

It's hard to find the time in the day
to make sure you're okay as well,
instead of focusing on the new love of your life.

You could put her in her crib when she naps
but you might miss the days
when she wants to nap in your arms.

You could let her cry while you make yourself breakfast,
but every time she even whimpers
a sliver cracks through your heart.

You could do a lot of things
but all you want to do is make sure
your baby is okay,
even if that means
neglecting yourself
a little bit.

And as you think
of all these things
instead of showering or napping
or anything you need to do,
you can hear her waking
and it's time to change her.

No one understands
the newfound fear
I have of nighttime.

How when the sun starts to set,
pure dread
cements in my stomach.

People ask me why I feel this way
and I don't even know how to explain.

I just know
that when it gets dark
so does my mind
and I barely survive
the night.

"You just don't understand how I feel." she cries to him.

"Then make me understand." he says.

But I can't.

I can't do this anymore.
They're better without me.
I have to leave.

I packed a suitcase
and I looked at my sleeping family
and I shed a few tears
and I thought
this is goodbye.

And then my baby woke.
And she didn't even cry.
She met my eyes,
as if she knew.
I ran to her
and cradled her in my arms.

Just this last time, I thought.

I rocked her back to sleep
and kissed her perfect head
and lied her back down in her bassinet,
and sat on my bed
and stared at her.

I promised myself that tomorrow I'd leave,
but she could use me here
for just tonight.

When the sun rose
the next morning
I knew I needed help.

Something is not right.

You are a good mama. You are a good mama.

Who even am I anymore?
I am a mother and a wife
and a woman and a friend
and a person and a stranger
and a human.

I am a human.

But who am I besides all that?

Am I still the woman who loves to read,
even though I haven't picked a book up in months?
Am I still the woman who laughs at dumb jokes,
even though I can't find my voice anymore?
Am I still the woman I used to be?

I am a mother now
and my world revolves around this tiny being
and I love this baby so much

but who am *I?*

I was skeptical to take
the little blue pill
that was supposed to take
my bad feelings away.

I'm glad I did,
because I'm still here.

I have to set an alarm on my phone
to remember to eat.

I have to let someone hold the baby
so I can shower.

I have to leave the house
by myself
for even five minutes.

I have to learn to take care of myself again
(even if I cry the entire time)
and I am starting today.

Sometimes I feel as if I am a failure as a mom.

What if I'm not doing this whole thing right?
Was your bottle the right temperature?
Do I bathe you enough?
Do I show you I love you enough?
I know I cry a lot,
and get frustrated,
but I promise it's not you.
I know I can always be better,
but will I ever be the perfect mother for you?

I cry in my room
as I watch you sleep peacefully.
Do you know how much I love you?
Do you know how much I hope
I am the mother that you deserve?
I will do anything I can
to be the mother you deserve.
Will I ever be the best mother I can for you?

… and then you open your tiny eyes
and I see the way you look at me,
and I feel your love

and it makes me feel
as if I've done everything right in the world.

I always thought it was ridiculous when I was told
"You don't know true love until you have kids."

At that point,
I didn't even know
if I wanted to have children
and you're telling me
if I don't,
I won't know true love?

Then I became a parent and I finally understood.

And how...

how
how
how

can I ever put the love I feel into words?
Could I explain how my life
has so much more meaning?

How they were right.
I didn't know this form of love,
the truest and purest and most unconditional.

I never knew true love
until I saw tiny hands grab my index finger
until I made bottles at 3am
until I went into a nursery and calmed a screaming baby
just by holding her
until I saw a black-and-white blob on a screen
and was told *there's your baby*
until I watched my body change
until I lie naked on a table,
throwing up and shaking uncontrollably,
as an entire medical team cut open my stomach
and handed a swaddled infant to my husband
and I thought *there's my baby*

until I looked at her
and she looked at me
and knew I would do anything
in my power
to give her the best life,
do it right
so that she won't ever have to worry
if she is loved enough

Baby
you are *so so so so* loved enough.

I guess I will give it to them, then – they were right.

I didn't know true love until you.

The days are long
and by nighttime I am so ready
for baby to be in bed
asleep
so I can be alone
for once in the day
my boobs aching
and my head hurting
and my body just needing to sit down
for one second.

And then the time comes
and I can see you on the monitor
snoring away,
finally getting my break…

and I miss you and wish you were awake.

The family members
who were never kind to me
love my daughter
and treat her the way I always wished to be,
and it hurts me
knowing that I wasn't worthy
of the love
that was there the whole time.

Nothing brings me the most pride or joy
than when my sweet baby is crying
and all it takes is my arms
to calm her.

The look in her eyes
when she finds out
Mama is here, and she is safe.

"Honey, if we have another baby,
you will be the one nursing."

Something I tease my husband about daily.

I struggle to love this new body
that did the unthinkable
just because I think
it doesn't look as desirable.

I sit down and notice
the little pouch of fat
that sits below my belt
and cringe.

People all around me
remind me
that I grew a baby
and I gave birth
and it's perfectly normal
and okay
and even beautiful
that my body isn't the same.

And I know they are right,
but that doesn't make it
much easier...

Changing diapers aren't as bad when it's your baby...

who am I kidding,
baby poop is still gross.

Google History

What is cradle cap?
Why does my baby sleep weird
Baby pausing breathing at night
How many wet diapers should a baby have a day
Do I have mastitis?
Easy meals for new moms
Signs of RSV
I think I hate my husband
DoorDash coupons
Happy movies for sad days
Why do we need money to survive
Do I have a clogged duct
Is my baby sleeping too much?
When do babies sleep through the night?
My baby hasn't pooped in 5 days
Divorce stats after new baby
Why does my baby spit up so much
Crockpot meals
PPD
Divorce lawyers
Do I have baby blues or PPD
Is the formula shortage over
Milk supply boosters
New mom support
Why having an only child is the best
Will I feel like myself again after having a baby?

Just wait until it's 3:04am
and you're yawning
as your baby drinks a bottle,
rocking him or her in your arms,
and humming random songs that come to mind.

As your little love falls asleep,
stare at their perfect face
and know that you are their warmth,
their home, their safety, their peace.

Nothing could replace the wonderful mother that is you.
You are perfect for your child.

No matter what that silly brain of yours thinks.

I could get up.

I could gently lie you in your crib
and tiptoe out of your room.

I could shut the door and get some housework done,
or even make a coffee and enjoy it while it's warm,
reading a book on the couch.

I could get so much done…
but I don't want to.

I look at your peacefully sleeping face
and realize time is going way too fast.

Months have passed since you were born,
how is that even possible?
Your once tiny hands
that you couldn't even wiggle
now grip my shirt tightly.

Your once bare eyelids
are decorated with
the longest and prettiest lashes I've ever seen.

Your cheeks are rosier,
you are bigger,
You're getting older.
You're my baby
but you're growing up.

And time isn't kind; it will only keep going.
I will only watch you get bigger
and taller
and smarter
and older…

and so, today, I won't worry about the things that can happen
tomorrow.
Or the next day.
Or the next.
Right now, I will be grateful
that you are mine
and I am yours.
I will sit here and rock you
as you nap in my arms,
knowing one day
I will wish for this moment once more.

I am learning to love myself
so that when my daughter is here,
she will see a woman
who admires her flaws
and appreciates her blemishes
and loves them just the same
as the pretty and desirable parts of her.

I will love myself
so that my daughter
won't have to learn
the hard way
what hating your body
and nitpicking your soul
does to you.

Instead,
she won't have to learn
what loving herself is.

She just will.

I see the way your father looks at you
and I never knew I could love him even more.

You have not only made me love you immensely,
but I am falling deeper in love with your daddy, too.

You are such a little blessing,
changing us all.

Being a mother was always in the cards for me.
I would look at babies
and feel that pull of love,
that want, that need.

I wanted to be a mother *so bad,*
to have a child of my own,
a part of me
and the person I love most.
Something to love and help grow
and to give the best life possible.

I never truly understood
what being a mother actually was
until I became one.

I am a mother which means
I will sacrifice everything
just to see their smile.
I will sacrifice everything
just to make sure they're okay.
I will sacrifice everything
my money my heirlooms my life
just to make sure
they are safe.

I am a mother
and I will do everything in my power
even tear the clothes off my back
to give them the life they deserve.

It was my choice to bring them into this world;
I will make sure they have the best life I can give them.

You've started smiling
and have little laughs.
You're so close to rolling over
and hitting every milestone.

I can't believe I blinked.

Our love has changed over the years.

What once was staying up late
and texting each other sweet words
towns and beds apart,
became sleeping next to each other every night
and snuggling as we fell asleep.

No longer were we clutching phones
anxiously waiting for a response
and fighting sleep,
but now we held each other,
our breathing in sync,
our legs intertwined.

Now our love is taking turns
trying to rock the baby to sleep
when we are both exhausted.

Now our love is
you washing my breast pump parts
and me kissing you goodnight at 3am.

Our love is no longer
cooking elaborate meals
but heating up the same large pizza
three nights in a row.

Our love is more of a survival right now
as we give our all to this tiny being we created.

But it's still our love.

Our love may not be spontaneous and romantic
like it once was,
but we still kiss good morning
and still text *I love you.*

And I know our love will change

again and again as we grow older,
and change as our seasons of life do,
and while I don't know where we will be in time,
I know I will always
kiss you good morning
and text you *I love you.*

I traded sleeping in
for early morning playdates
and going out with friends
for quiet nights after the baby is asleep.

I traded in fast food and quick dinners
to cleaning fresh fruit and veggies
and cooking healthy meals almost every night.

I used to spoil myself with whatever I wanted,
and now I give my child the world.

I'm grateful for my memories
but I don't regret my choices at all,
I love this new season of life
and I'm so happy I became a mama.

Someday I will tell my baby
about the baby before her.
The one that we never met,
who died in my belly
just five short weeks after living.

I will explain
why one day a year
I don't want to get out of bed,
why I cry so much more than I usually do.
I will tell her why that name is so dear to us,
who it belongs to.
I will tell her why we celebrate
a random Tuesday in July
and why I have that tattoo.

I will tell her of the baby before her
and I know that she will love him
just as much as we do.

I have never felt more pride
than when I look at you growing
and know
it's all because
of me.

That when you were in my body
I grew you
from a minuscule cell
and nourished you
into an
8lb 4oz baby.

And now
I watch you nurse
and I see you grow
and thrive
and change
and I know
it's all because of *me*
and my milk
and my body.

IN THE EYES OF A FATHER

She is different.

The person sitting next to me
rocking her baby
isn't the same woman
I married years ago.

There's something about her that I cannot even explain.

She is braver. She is stronger.
She has stopped worrying
about what people think of her.
She is more patient than I've ever seen
and she smiles brighter
and cries more often.
She has stopped questioning her worth
and has started believing in herself.
She doesn't mind the smaller things
that used to make us fight,
and she worries about us more
and I can tell she is happier than ever.

Oh, how I love to see her so happy.

She loves me still
but I can feel
that with this baby in her arms
she loves me even more.

She is still my love. She is still my wife.
But now she is a mother.

I know that I have done
many great things in this life
and I will do many more,
but I am confident in the fact
that you are my absolute greatest accomplishment.

One of my favorite things
is when you're playing with your toys
and get so in the zone
you forget I'm there,
until suddenly your head snaps up
and you meet my gaze
and you smile so wide
when you realize
I am still with you.

I will always be here, baby.

You snuggle me on the couch
and I hold your hand
and I pray that we will always have
moments like these.

Like even when you're grown up
and your tiny hand is bigger,
you still might want to hold mine for a second or two.

Like even when I kiss you goodbye,
you will smile with your dimples
and I will kiss both of them.

Like even when you're grown up,
you'll still be my baby
and I will remember the tiniest hand
that once didn't fit in mine.

They say
when a baby giggles,
a fairy is born.

I can only imagine
the multitude of fairies
that you have created,
my sweet love.

I struggle with who I am now.
The clothes in my closet feel weird on me.
How can they
accurately represent who I am
when I am a whole new person?

I look at the body that is mine yet doesn't belong to me.
The once perky boobs that are full of milk
and sag towards my belly button.
The stomach that is flabby
and painted with red and brown and purple stripes.
The long scar at the bottom of my abdomen
that is slowly healing.

She feels familiar in a way
but also totally alien.

I know this is my body
but it's so different.

I used to be one way
and then I got pregnant
and slowly became another
and now that baby is out
and my body is new once more.

I am proud of this body and what she has done for me,
even if it's taking me a while to convince myself.

I want to love every ounce of myself
because I want my baby to grow up
and never doubt the things that look different than others.

She won't look at my body and see problems,
she will look at my body and see *mama.*

When she has the same "blemishes"
she won't look at them in disgust,
but will say "I'm beautiful like mama."

I cannot be the best mother for you
if I am not the best person for me.

I am doing things that make me happy
and taking breaks from you
and I am not feeling guilty about it.

I'm enjoying hobbies
and I'm missing you, of course,
but when I get back home
I can love you even better.

I will not feel guilty
for taking care of myself
so I can take better care of you.

The first time you said it
I'm pretty sure it was an accident,
but I proudly boasted anyway,
telling everyone who would listen
about you saying your first word.

Now, I hear you say it
and when I look at you,
you are looking back at me.

"What?" I ask.

You smile and start crawling toward me,
and you say it again.

You know who I am,
and I love hearing that word
escape your lips.

"Mama!"

Being a mother is so hard.
It's so unbelievably hard.
Not only the things that you see—
constantly feeding the baby,
changing the baby,
loving the baby,
but everything else, too.

Like scheduling doctor's appointments
and taking off work to go.
Like laundry
endless laundry
that eventually you put away when she outgrows.
Or do you sell it to make extra money,
because diapers are expensive?
But what if you have another baby, shouldn't you keep it?
And then bath time.
And medicine.
And rocking her just the way she likes it
while watching the clock,
because if she falls asleep in your arms
she will wake in her crib,
but if you don't rock her long enough
she will just cry.
And trying to understand what exactly she wants
because you've given her snacks and toys and
she is still crying
she is still crying
and now you're crying.
And knowing that even when you cry
it's all on you.
You have to wipe your tears
and keep on going
because you're mom
and no one understand that
better than a mother.

When I was pregnant,
I used to cry in your arms,
fearing that I would miss
when it was just us two.

We've lived this life together for years
just us two
doing what we want,
like going to eat pancakes at 10pm because *why not*
and lying in bed all day because *why not*
and taking impromptu trips because we could and because *why not.*

I was terrified I would hate our new life
and the inability to do whatever we wanted,
and planning our life around someone totally new.

But here we are
now us three.

Our life may be different
but I don't even miss
the *we* we used to be
because I love the *we* we are now.

We watch baby TV instead of movies we like,
but smile at each other over the top of her head.
We giggle at baby pictures in bed after she is asleep
because we miss her *so much.*
We rush to get her out of bed in the mornings
and are so excited to spend another day together.

Our new life together is different
but I wouldn't change it for the world.

I love being *us three.*

Your tiny newborn fingers
have become toddler fingers
and I tear up every time I see them.

The toys you used to love
now are in the donate bin.

You are smarter than them now,
and I can't believe it.

Two months ago you could barely grab anything
and now you're throwing things, shaking rattles, and more.

Watching you grow and learn–
My God, you are so smart and brave–
fills me simultaneously with
pride and heartbreak.

You say mama & smile
and I love that you can,
but wasn't it only moments ago
you looked at me for the first time?

The day has finally come
where you don't need me
to rock you to sleep anymore.

You prefer when I lie you down
and pat your back,
tell you I love you
and leave the room.

You will get comfortable on your own
and fall asleep alone.

It breaks this mama's heart
because I remember
when you could only ever sleep in my arms,
and now here you are,
getting so big.

I never knew how well I could know a person until you.

I know that when you rub your eyes
it means it's time to sleep.
I know the way you cry can mean
you're hungry or just want me.
I know that when you laugh
it's more a chuckle than a giggle,
you frown when you're mad
but happy you loves to wiggle.

You have the sweetest, stinkiest grin
and I can tell when you're done eating.
You dance when I sing to you
and love to interrupt my reading.
I know the way you love me,
with hugs and slobbery kisses
and don't ever forget I love you so much.
Now please let me wash the dishes.

She is so far from glamorous.

She has been wearing the same sweatpants
for three days
(at least),
and she's covered in milk and snot and crumbs.

Daily makeup and showers
have been replaced
with half-assed washings
from baby baths
and *did I forget to brush my teeth again?*

And yet,
he tells her
this is the most beautiful
he's ever seen her.

She knows he's lying,
but she loves him anyway.

You used to be so tiny in this car seat.

You used to barely fit, it seems.
Gently buckle you in
try not to hurt you.

Take you out of this hospital brand-new
and drive slowly down the highway
with your tiny hand holding onto my finger.

Now I look at you
and you're almost too big.
The new car seat we bought
is in the box,
waiting to be assembled in the car.

I know it's time to say goodbye
to this tiny car seat,
but I am not ready.

I sometimes miss drinking hot coffee
and sleeping in,
but then I see your little brown curls
and watch you admire the sunrise,
and even though
it's 7am
and my coffee is lukewarm,
I'm happier now
than I've ever been.

The baby monitor lights up.
You are up from your nap!
I watch as you sit up
and rub your eyes.

My favorite part is next.

I slowly open your bedroom door
and walk inside,
saying
"Hi, sweetie!"
and when you see me
your face lights up
in the sweetest grin.
"Mama!"
you say,
reaching for me.

I pick you up and kiss your cheek.
I will never ever *ever* forget moments like these.

Your hair is finally starting to grow back
and it sticks up all over your head–
this way and that,
curls here and there.

My little Danny DeVito.

There will never be enough time
to kiss your chunky cheeks
or snuggle you close to me.
I cry when I think about how fast you grow
and how unfair it is
that I can't be there to watch you every second.
I must go to work and make money
for us to survive,
when all I want to do
is be with you.
Because even when I'm living away from you, I'm not really
living,
just walking and talking until I'm back home
and I'm alive again,
fueled by your giggles
and the way you say "Mama."

I am annoyed that you woke up again
this is the third time tonight–it's 3:47am.
Tomorrow is going to be a struggle.

I rock you in my arms
and you hold my shirt
and suck on your binky
as you fall asleep.

And all the annoyance
(okay, most of it)
floods out of my body
as I watch you drift away.

You don't sleep in my arms anymore–
you've outgrown that.
It's been weeks since we've rocked like this,
and you snored against my chest.

Even though I wish it wasn't at 3:47am
this sweet moment
reminds me of the little things
I take for granted.

I think it is the sweetest, most ironic thing
how to me
you've always been
my little blueberry,
and now
it's the snack
you whine for every day.

You'd eat an entire basket if you could.

I have never loved anything
so wholeheartedly and so fiercely
until I met you.

I love your daddy
with all my heart
but there is something about the way
I love you.

We have been together through it all.

Morning sickness
(and afternoon and night sickness),
swollen ankles
and endless milkshakes.

They cut me open
to get you
and you were there
while they stitched me back up,
wide eyed
and lying next to me.

We were together the entire first few months.
You sleeping in a bassinet
just an arm's reach away,
me nursing you every few hours
and changing you the same.

I see you grow
every single day.

I look into your eyes
(the color a mix between your daddy's and I)
and I see my adoration
reflecting back.

Even though you can't say it yet,
I know you feel the exact same way.

If there's one thing I've learned
most above the rest,
there's no bond stronger
than the one between
baby and mama.

I will never be the same woman again,
and I am okay with that.

I like this new version of me a lot better.

I blinked and the baby is ten months old.
I can't even tell you what happened
when she was six months or younger.
I was just trying to survive,
and I'm sad I don't remember.

Of course I remember some things—
the tiny baby cries and the nursing all night,
even baby snuggles and sleeping when I could.

But it's all blurred together in one long long *long* day.

Survival mode.

I have learned
how easy it is
to love my daughter.

How even when she cries all night
or makes a mess
or spits up all over,
or worse,

I still love her more than anything.

I was always told
I hope you have a child like you
and made to seem
like I was so hard to love,
and I don't understand why,
because here I am
with a child like me
and it is so damn easy.

I look at you and wonder
how something so perfect,
so sweet,
so lovable and unique
and amazing came from me.

You are brave and kind
and you speak your mind.
You are smart
and laugh loudly
and are *you* proudly.

You have shown me
these qualities
I adore in you
have actually been hiding
inside of me
this entire time.

Thank you
for helping me
love myself a little bit more.

The Mother's Love is

Sucking the hair and dirt off a pacifier before giving it back
Rocking a baby to sleep for hours
Always eating cold food because she's too busy feeding
everyone else
Picking up the same toys even though she knows they'll get
thrown off the table again
Watching the same movie 10x in a row because it's their favorite
Happily disinfecting toys covered in oatmeal residue
Picking tiny noses
Tattoos of baby names
That birth scar
Unconditional & never-ending

I am a goddess of life,
a creator of souls.

I am filled with magic
and power
and the stardust
of sunshine
flows through my veins.

A LETTER TO MY RAINBOW BABY

When I found out I was pregnant with you,
I was not overjoyed.
I was not as excited as I should've been,
nor could I believe it.
I took two tests a day
to make sure I was correct -
that, yes, I was actually pregnant again.

But I had been pregnant for a while before.
And then I wasn't
as my body ripped him away from me.
It happened so suddenly,
realizing that my baby died inside of me.
A miscarriage, they said.
It's common, they said.

And that was it.

I had a miscarriage,
took two days to be sad,
and then was back at work
and continuing life,
even though I felt dead inside.

And then, months later, pregnant again.

I dreaded each new day,
waiting for the worst to happen.
I made it to five weeks pregnant,
then six,
then ten,
then thirteen.

With each little milestone
and passing week
I started feeling a little more relaxed…
but not *too* relaxed

because I couldn't give my fear away.

I was happily pregnant before
but I lost that baby.

Maybe if I get too happy this time
I will lose you too?

Our sonogram appointment came and I saw you.
A little blob on a screen.
You were there and you were healthy.
You were growing and okay.

You were okay yet I couldn't love you.
I wouldn't allow myself to feel the joy in growing you.
I woke up each day
still worried that this was too good to be true,
that you'd leave soon.

And then I felt that first kick.
I knew you were there.
You were safe and okay,
just like the doctor said.

(But what if they were lying?
You could be safe now
but that could change in a heartbeat.)

I only allowed myself a tiny sliver of love.

I could only love you enough
that it wouldn't hurt if I lost you.
Because If I loved you too much and you died,
I don't know if I could survive.

I would love you in your little kicks
and then love you when I thought of you,
but only in those fleeting moments,
because getting attached could be fatal for both of us.

Finally the day came when it was time for you to arrive.
Even as we sat in the hospital together
I knew I wouldn't be free from fear
until you were safely in my arms.

And then... *there you were.*

Two eyes. A button nose.
A dark head of hair and a perfect newborn cry.
You are real and are beautiful
and you are my baby and I am your mother.

And here we are now.

You made it and are safe
and I love you so much more
than I ever thought possible.
You make my life meaningful
and I cannot ever imagine you not being here.

But as much as I love you,
my sweet rainbow,
it's still unfair.

I hate that I had to lose a baby
to gain another.
I wish I could've had both of you,
but I also know that if I never lost the baby before,
I might not have you now.

What an impossible trade.

We talk about the joys of rainbows
but don't see the repercussions
of what the rain before has caused.

Just because I have my rainbow
doesn't lessen the pain of the storm.

I still miss my baby and cry for them
while being grateful for the baby crying in my arms.
I just hold on to the hope
that we will all be together someday,
and my heart will finally be complete
with both of my babies next to me.

For now, I will hug you more often.
I will watch you play and sing and dance.
I will kiss you goodnight each night
and kiss you good morning each morning.
I will love you a little more each day,
and even more the next.
I am grateful you're my rainbow
and know my life wouldn't be complete without you.
I will admire your colors and embrace your joy,
because you are my baby,
and I am your mother.

Every baby is different,
and that is perfectly okay.

You don't compare
the sprouting wildflowers,
do you?

I am a jungle gym
and a tissue
a toy holder
and a snack dispenser
a dairy cow
and healing kisses
a chef
and a tickle monster
a librarian
and a snuggler.

I am a mother
and all of these things
at once.

I am reminding myself that the little things don't matter.
I can buy used clothes and toys.
I don't have to clean every day.
I don't have to always plan outside activities.
I can make mac n cheese for dinner three nights in a row.
I can get a babysitter and go out.

I don't have to pressure myself to be a perfect mom, because
there is no such thing.

My baby won't look back and remember all these things.

She will remember
being played with
warm clothes
her favorite broken toy
yummy dinner every night
new friends
and a mama who did her best
and who loved her the whole time.

She will remember being loved.
And that's the most important thing.

Mama, it'll get easier.

When the baby starts sleeping longer.
When the baby can entertain himself.
When the baby can grab her pacifier
and put it back in her mouth.
When the baby can sit up without help.
When the baby can smile at you.
When the baby gets older
and is a little human
instead of a potato.

It'll get easier.
You got this.

I am encountering magic for the first time again.
Through your eyes I see what you do–
how exciting it is when it rains,
what it's like to see something sparkle,
watching me make dinner
and tasting ice cream for the first time ever.

These mundane things I've done for years
you are just now experiencing,
and it's reminding me just how special living is,
just how special *being alive* is.
You have made me appreciate
the little things I used to ignore,
and there you go giggling at the bird
that flew past the window,
and I love the sound and the life that you give me.

You bounce in place
as music plays
and laugh along
to the lights on your toy.

I smile at you
from across the room.

These are the moments
no one prepares you for,
but they become
the most memorable.

I hope to never forget these Thursday mornings.

"Will I ever be a good enough mother for you?"
I whisper against your hair,
holding you on a Saturday morning.

You turn to smile at me
with that two-toothed grin,
and even though you cannot talk,
I know exactly what you are saying.

"Mama, you already are and more."

I don't give myself enough credit.
I grew an entire *life* inside of me.
Day by day for months,
I kept a baby safe
as it grew
from a poppyseed to a watermelon.
I gave birth to you
and took care of you
on three hours of sleep
while healing my body
and learning how to be your mom.
I fed you and clothed you
and protected you
and bathed you
and loved you
and I still do these things
every single day.

I am powerful,
and that is putting it lightly.

I will never forget
all the firsts
we've shared together.

Your first laugh
brought on by a Valentines day balloon.
The first time you smiled
brought on
by me being silly.
When you first rolled over... off the couch.
(Yeah, not my best parenting moment).
Trying your first food - mushy bananas!
You crawling to me
and my scooping you in my arms.
When you got your first cold
and I worried all night.
When you got your first shots
and I cried with you.
Your first word
Mama.
Your first time saying dada, kitty, and whoa!
The first time I held you.
And the most recent,
the first time you stood on your own
and your dad and I were staring at you,
will she take a few steps?

You haven't yet,
but I know there's only a matter of time.

All these firsts in just this one year.
I cannot wait to see
all the other firsts
that will come next year.

L oving you is my favorite thing to do
Y ou will always be my baby
L ife before you is something I don't miss
A nd I will promise I will always be
H ere ; your mother, your biggest supporter, and your home.

I feel like myself again

s l o w l y
              and
                  s l o w l y

I'm putting mascara on in the mornings
and I'm making time for myself
brushing my teeth daily again
and wearing clothes that make me feel good.

I read between naps
and take baths after you're asleep.
I reheat my coffee and drink it warm.

These past two years
have been hard.
Pregnancy and then
surviving the fog
of early motherhood...

but here I am

s l o w l y

feeling like me again.

Standing on two wobbly legs
walking a few steps
and then falling down.

Now you are doing it all again.

I hope you will always be this brave.

This time has been so hard for us, and yet we are still together.

We have been going on date nights again
and making time for one another.
We've started completing puzzles
(when did we get so old?)
and snuggling on the couch
falling asleep
after the baby is in bed.

I love you so much
and I'm sorry if this year
I didn't show it that well,
but we've made it through survival mode
and now we can love each other again,
better than ever before.

Thank you for being there
during the hardest parts.
I love you.

I could listen to you babble for hours,
the sweet melody of nonsense
mixed with giggles and random screams,
making me smile all the time.

Becoming a mother has unlocked my power.
I am more confident now than ever.
I am braver and stronger
and smarter and happier
and sexier
and more capable
than I ever thought I was before

How is this
the last month
that you are considered an infant?

Next month you are a toddler
and I cannot believe it.

Wasn't it just yesterday you were born?
That we brought you home?
That I was waking every night
to feed you and rock you to sleep?
That you couldn't even move,
and now you're walking, playing?

I am planning your first birthday party
and family pictures
and starting to pack away bottles
and I can't believe
we are already to this point.

How are you almost one?

I am figuring out
who I am
in this new body of mine
and allowing myself
to enjoy
every second.

I am donating clothes
that don't fit me anymore,
and I am slowly rebuilding my closet
with fabrics
that make me feel
gorgeous and amazing.

Because I am
gorgeous and amazing.

I feed the baby dinner
while you draw her a bath.

I bathe her free of food and dirt
while you switch me and clean up dinner.

I dress her in jammies
while you heat her bottle.

I read her a book
while you hold her in your lap.

I kiss her goodnight
and you rock her to sleep.

When she is asleep,
you meet me on the couch.

We rest against each other
and giggle about how beautiful our baby is.

I turn on the TV
and we intertwine our legs.

After the day is over
and our baby is sleeping,
we finally return
to just me + you.

These are the moments
our love comes alive again.

I breastfed for one entire year.
365+ days.

Through clogged ducts
and painful pumps
and the early, bleeding latches
to the bitings
and the slow weaning
until the last drop of breastmilk was gone.

It's bittersweet
and yet, I'm ready for it to be over.
I look at my infant and know
that she got here because of me.

I am so proud of myself and my body.

I always had this fear

of losing myself when I had a child.

I don't want to be *just* a mother.
I am so much more.
I am a woman, a wife,
a person with big dreams
and bigger aspirations,
goals and plans and hobbies and more.

Then I had you and I realized
I didn't lose myself by becoming your mother,
I found another piece of myself
that I can proudly add to the kaleidoscope of who I am.

DEAR MAMA

I know you don't feel appreciated. Believe me, I feel the same
sometimes.
We bust our asses and do everything.
If we weren't here the family would collapse, kids wouldn't eat
dinner, laundry wouldn't get done, bills wouldn't get paid,
doctors appointments wouldn't get made...
I could go on and on and on.

Listen to me.

YOU ARE INCREDIBLE.
YOU ARE MAGICAL.
YOU ARE ENOUGH
YOU ARE BEAUTIFUL.
YOU ARE STRONG.

You took a tiny cell
and grew it in your womb
and made it an actual human being.

A HUMAN.
WITH EYES AND TOES
AND ORGANS AND A VOICE
AND A LIFE OF THEIR OWN.

Do not ever for one second think
you are anything short of amazing, unbelievable, incredible.
You did the unimaginable.
YOU DID.
Not your partner,
YOU.

Being a mother is so important, I know,
but it's okay to also be a person.
A woman.

I want you to remember today and every day

that you deserve to be happy
and you deserve to be loved
and you deserve to take breaks
and you deserve to do whatever you need for yourself.

Your baby loves you.
Your children love you.
You are so loved by everyone else,
and I need you to love yourself the same.

This is your baby's life, yes,
and we have to sacrifice for them, of course,
but you don't have to fade to the background
and be forgotten.

Stand TALL.
Be PROUD of who you are
and what you've done.

Your child will grow up and look at you and think
Wow, my mom is so amazing
and they will be inspired by you
to be amazing, too.

So, I know.
I know you're tired.
But you're still doing the damn thing.
You're still going
and you deserve to take a break and rest
and you deserve to have help
and you deserve to have hobbies
and you deserve to go out sometimes
and you deserve to do what you want
and you deserve to love yourself
and your life
as much as you love
your baby.

Do not settle for anything less

look in that mirror
and be proud of you,
because you
are one badass, beautiful,
amazing and magical woman.

And one badass, beautiful,
amazing and magical mother.

A year ago
I was bouncing on an exercise ball,
drinking raspberry tea,
taking walks,
and eating pineapple
to encourage you
to make your arrival.

Now here I am
hanging up streamers
and baking your birthday cake.

My, how time flies.

OUR FIRST YEAR

I am so proud of who you are
and who you've become
in such little time.

Only a year ago
you could barely move
or see
or do anything other than
eat, sleep, cry.

Now here you are,
clapping and laughing,
playing and crawling,
taking your first steps
and saying little words.

You recognize sounds
and people
and are silly and lovely
and amazing and sweet.

You have brought so much joy
and love
and happiness
into my life.

You have changed me,
and you have made me realize
how amazing I am.

I have learned how precious and strong my body is.

How sometimes all you need
is a big hug to make the day all better.
How I've learned patience and kindness
and so much love just from a rocking chair at 2am.

I have learned that my needs matter
and I'm still the amazing woman I was
before becoming a mother.
(but now even more so).

I have learned
what true love is
and that my world resides
in a pair of blue eyes.

I have learned so much
just in this past year
and I cannot wait to see
you grow and change
and bloom even wilder
next year

and the next year

and the next...

CHEYENNE BLUETT

XOXO

ACKNOWLEDGEMENTS

Thank you to my husband for being my biggest supporter, my sexiest muse, and my best friend.

Thank you to my daughter who changed my world. You completed me.

Thank you to my family and friends for your love and for believing in me.

And last, thank you to my readers who let me have the coolest job in the world.

CHEYENNE BLUETT

ABOUT THE AUTHOR:

Cheyenne Bluett was born and raised in Illinois, where she still currently resides with her husband, fur-children, and human daughter. When she is not writing or working on one of her ten thousand projects, you can find her snuggling her daughter, reading a good book with a hot chocolate, or rewatching Twilight for the thousandth time.

connect with her on social media –

@theecheyennebluett

@cheyennebluettpoetry

www.cheyennebluett.com

CHEYENNE BLUETT

CAN YOU HELP?

Thank You For Reading My Book!

I really appreciate all of your feedback, and I love hearing what you have to say.

Please leave me a review on Amazon letting me know what you thought of the book.

Thank you so much!

Xoxo,

Cheyenne